The King and His Wish

Written by Alison Hawes

Illustrated by Kate Slater

OXFORD
UNIVERSITY PRESS

The King had a wish.

I wish to
go up!

The King got a big, red box.

5

8

But you will fall!

And he fell with a ...

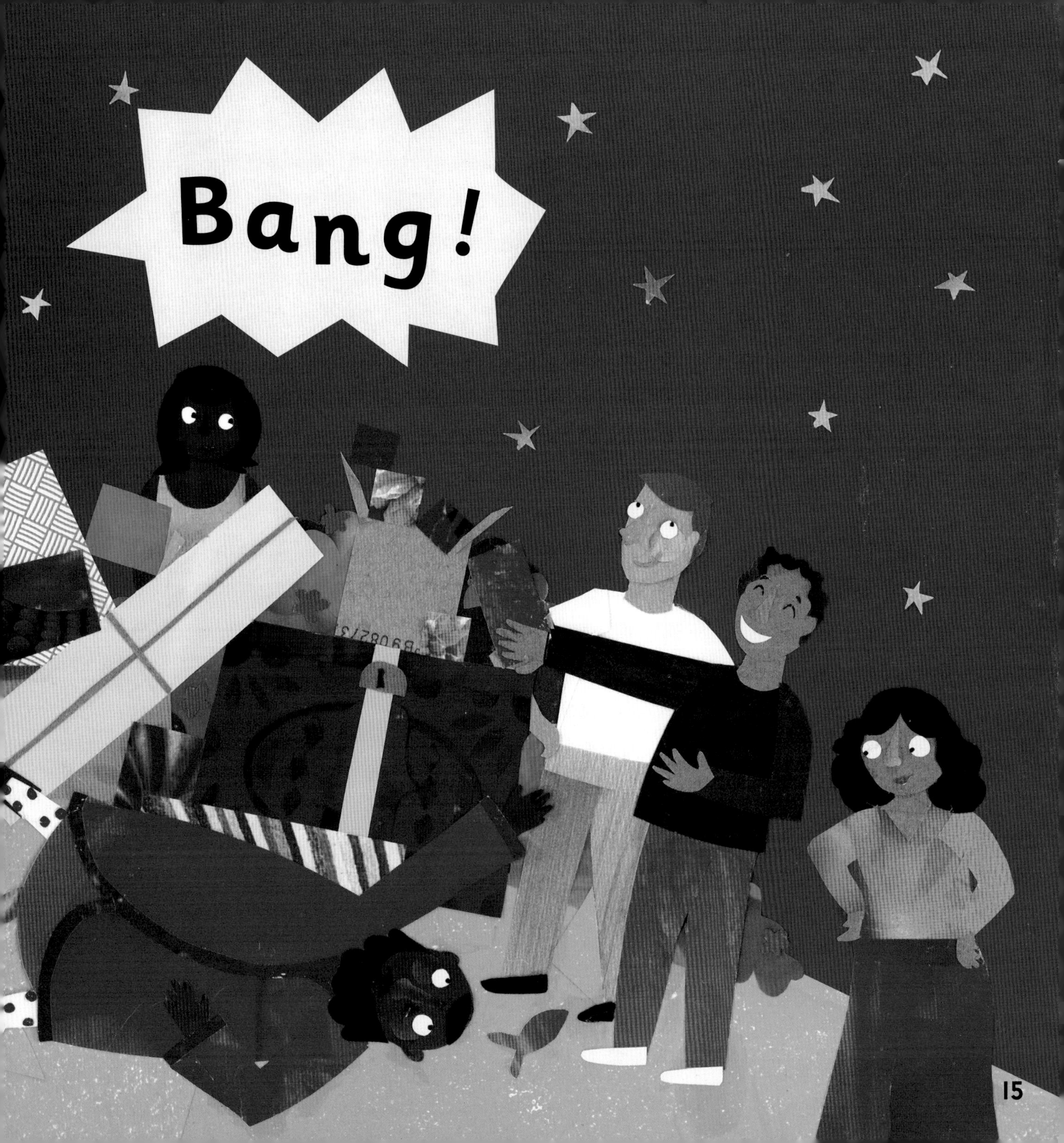
Bang!

Retell the story

Once upon a time...

The end.